Principles of Democracy:

The Constitution and The Bill of Rights

edited by Ellen Hansen

©Discovery Enterprises, Ltd.
Carlisle, Massachusetts

ISBN 1-878668-53-6 paperback edition
Library of Congress Catalog Card Number 95-68769

10 9 8 7 6 5 4 3 2 1

Printed in the United States of America

Subject Reference Guide

Principles of Democracy:
The Constitution and The Bill of Rights
edited by Ellen Hansen

Constitution of the United States

The Bill of Rights

Constitutional Convention

James Madison

Photo Credits

Independence Hall (p. 24),
"The Signing of the Constitution" (p. 33),
Portrait of James Madison by Gilbert Stuart (p. 39),
George Mason (p. 46).
Courtesy: Library of Congress.

Page from Convention Journal Records "The Great Compromise" (p. 43), Courtesy: National Archives.

Table of Contents

"If men were angels,
no government would be necessary.
If angels were to govern men . . .
no controls on government would
be necessary."

— James Madison

Foreword

> WE THE PEOPLE of the United States, in order to form a more perfect Union, establish justice, insure domestic tranquility, provide for the common defense, promote the general welfare, and secure the blessings of liberty to ourselves and our posterity, do ordain and establish this Constitution for the United States of America.

These words lead us into a remarkable document: the U.S. Constitution. Neither long nor overly complex, our Constitution provides the flexible foundation necessary to a country as vast and diverse as ours.

Each generation of Americans rediscovers the safeguards of the Constitution in action. Whether facing the Civil War, a World War, an economic depression, segregation, or freedom of speech issues, we benefit from the Constitution's built-in checks and balances between the powers of the executive, legislative, and judicial branches of government.

Our right to vote means we can effect governmental change by voting in a new president or new legislators. The Constitution even provides for a way to amend, or change, itself. In fact, the states ratified (approved) the first ten amendments within a few years of ratifying the Constitution. Those first ten amendments, known as the Bill of Rights, protect important individual rights. There are currently twenty-seven amendments to the Constitution.

This book examines the people and the process involved in composing our Constitution. Fifty-five delegates attended the Federal Convention in Philadelphia during the hot, humid months of May through September, 1787. Of the thirteen states, only Rhode Island failed to appoint delegates. Who were these men, and what qualities did they bring to the task of founding a new nation? Let's take a look.

Note: The primary source material in this book retains the original spellings, and misspellings.

* in the text refers to notes on pp. 55-56.

Character Sketches of Delegates to the Federal Convention

Among the fifty-five delegates attending the Federal Convention, twenty-one had fought in the American Revolution, eight had signed the Declaration of Independence, and three-fourths of them had served in Continental Congresses. Many had helped write state constitutions, and served as members of state legislatures. Over half were lawyers; seven had been governors of their states; and others were merchants, planters, statesmen, clergy, judges, college professors, physicians, and shoemakers. In age, they ranged from men still in their 20's and 30's, up to Benjamin Franklin in his 80's.*

William Pierce, one of the delegates from Georgia, wrote character sketches of his colleagues. Here are some of his descriptions.

(From *The Records of the Federal Convention of 1787*, Max Farrand, ed. CT: Yale University Press, 1911)

. . . Mr. Gerry's character is marked for integrity and perseverance. He is a hesitating and laborious speaker;—possesses a great degree of confidence and goes extensively into all subjects that he speaks on, without respect to elegance or flower of diction. He is connected and sometimes clear in his arguments, conceives well, and cherishes as his first virtue, a love for his Country. Mr. Gerry is very much of a Gentleman in his principles and manners;—he has been engaged in the mercantile line and is a Man of property. He is about 37 years of age. . . .

Mr. Sherman exhibits the oddest shaped character I ever remember to have met with. He is awkward, unmeaning, and unaccountably strange in his manner. But in his train of thinking there is something regular, deep and comprehensive; yet the oddity of his address, the vulgarisms that accompany his public speaking, and that strange New England cant which runs through his public as well as his private speaking make everything that is connected with him grotesque and laughable;—and yet he deserves infinite praise,—no Man has a better Heart or a clearer Head. If he cannot embellish he can furnish thoughts that are wise and useful. He is an able politician, and extremely artful in accomplishing any particular object;—it is remarked that he seldom fails. I am told he sits on the Bench in Connecticut, and is very correct in the discharge of his Judicial functions. . . . He is about 60.

Mr. Elsworth is a Judge of the Supreme Court in Connecticut;—he is a Gentleman of a clear, deep, and copious understanding; eloquent, and connected in public debate; and always attentive to his duty. . . . Mr. Elsworth is about 37 years of age, a Man much respected for his integrity, and venerated for his abilities.

Colo. Hamilton is deservedly celebrated for his talents. He is a practitioner of the Law, and reputed to be a finished Scholar. . . . Colo. Hamilton requires time to think,—he enquires into every part of his subject with the searchings of phylosophy, and when he comes forward he comes highly charged with interesting matter, there is no skimming over the surface of a subject with him, he must sink to the bottom to see what foundation it rests on. . . . He is about 33 years old, of small stature, and lean. His manners are tinctured with stiffness, and sometimes with a degree of vanity that is highly disagreeable. . . .

Mr. Lansing is a practicing Attorney at Albany, and Mayor of that Corporation. He has a hesitation in his speech, that will prevent his being an Orator of any eminence;—his legal knowledge I am told is not extensive, nor his education a good one. He is however a Man of good sense, plain in his manners, and sincere in his friendships. He is about 32 years of age.

M. Patterson is one of those kind of Men whose powers break in upon you, and create wonder and astonishment. He is a Man of great modesty, with looks that bespeak talents of no great extent,—but he is a Classic, a Lawyer, and an Orator;—and of a disposition so favorable to his advancement that every one seemed ready to exalt him with their praises. He is very happy in the choice of time and manner of engaging in a debate, and never speaks but when he understands his subject well. This Gentleman is about 34 years of age, of a very low stature. . . .

Dr. Franklin is well known to be the greatest phylosopher of the present age;—all the operations of nature he seems to understand,—the very heavens obey him, and the Clouds yield up their Lightning to be imprisoned in his rod. But what claim he has to the politician, posterity must determine. . . . He is 82 years old, and possesses an activity of mind equal to a youth of 25 years of age. . . .

Robert Morris . . . [although] not learned, yet he is as great as those who are. I am told that when he speaks in the Assembly of Pennsylvania, that he bears down all before him. What could have been his reason for not Speaking in the Convention I know not,—but he never once spoke on any point. This Gentleman is about 50 years old. . . .

Mr. Wilson ranks among the foremost in legal and political knowledge. He has joined to a fine genius all that can set him off and show him to advantage. He is well acquainted with Man, and understands all the passions that influence him. Government seems to have been his peculiar Study, all the political institutions of the World he knows in detail, and can trace the causes and effects of every revolution from the earliest stages of the Greecian commonwealth down to the present time. No man is more clear, copious, and comprehensive than Mr. Wilson, yet he is no great Orator. He draws the attention not by the charm of his eloquence, but by the force of his reasoning. He is about 45 years old.

Mr. Governeur Morris is one of those Genius's in whom every species of talents combine to render him conspicuous and flourishing in public debate:—He winds through all the mazes of rhetoric, and throws around him such a glare that he charms, captivates, and leads away the senses of all who hear him. . . . But with all these powers he is fickle and inconstant, —never pursuing one train of thinking,—nor ever regular. He has gone through a very extensive course of reading, and is acquainted with all the sciences. No Man has more wit,—nor can any one engage the attention more than Mr. Morris. . . . This Gentleman is about 38 years old, he has been unfortunate in losing one of his Legs, and getting all the flesh taken off his right arm by a scald, when a youth.

Mr. Dickinson . . . I had often heard that he was a great Orator, but I found him an indifferent Speaker. With an affected air of wisdom he labors to produce a trifle,—his language is irregular and incorrect,—his flourishes (for he sometimes attempts them), are like expiring flames, they just shew themselves and go out;—no traces of them are left on the mind to chear or animate it. He is, however, a good writer and will ever be considered one of the most important characters in the United States. He is about 55 years old, and was bred a Quaker. . . .

List of Delegates Attending the Federal Convention

NEW HAMPSHIRE
- John Langdon
- Nicholas Gilman

MASSACHUSETTS
- Elbridge Gerry
- Nathaniel Gorham
- Rufus King
- Caleb Strong

RHODE ISLAND
- No delegates appointed

CONNECTICUT
- William Samuel Johnson
- Roger Sherman
- Oliver Ellsworth

NEW YORK
- Robert Yates
- Alexander Hamilton
- John Lansing, Junior

NEW JERSEY
- David Brearley
- William Churchill Houston
- William Paterson
- William Livingston
- Jonathan Dayton

PENNSYLVANIA
- Thomas Mifflin
- Robert Morris
- George Clymer
- Jared Ingersoll
- Thomas Fitzsimons
- James Wilson
- Gouverneur Morris
- Benjamin Franklin

DELAWARE
- George Read
- Gunning Bedford, Junior

DELAWARE (cont.)
- John Dickinson
- Richard Bassett
- Jacob Broom

MARYLAND
- James McHenry
- Daniel of St. Thomas Jenifer
- Daniel Carroll
- John Francis Mercer
- Luther Martin

VIRGINIA
- George Washington
- Edmund Randolph
- John Blair
- James Madison, Junior
- George Mason
- George Wythe
- James McClurg

NORTH CAROLINA
- Alexander Martin
- William Richardson Davie
- Richard Dobbs Spaight
- William Blount
- Hugh Williamson

SOUTH CAROLINA
- John Rutledge
- Charles Pinckney
- Charles Cotesworth Pinckney
- Pierce Butler

GEORGIA
- William Few
- Abraham Baldwin
- William Pierce
- William Houstoun

Mr. Jenifer is a Gentleman of fortune in Maryland;—he is always in good humour, and never fails to make his company pleased with him. He sits silent in the Senate, and seems to be conscious that he is no politician. From his long continuance in single life, no doubt but he has made the vow of celibacy. He speaks warmly of the Ladies notwithstanding. Mr. Jenifer is about 55 years of Age, and once served as an Aid de Camp to Major Genl. Lee. . . .

Genl. Washington is well known as the Commander in chief of the late American Army. Having conducted these states to independence and peace, he now appears to assist in framing a Government to make the People happy. . . . The General was conducted to the Chair as President of the Convention by the unanimous voice of its Members. He is in the 52d. year of his age. . . .

Mr. Mason is a Gentleman of remarkable strong powers, and possesses a clear and copious understanding. He is able and convincing in debate, steady and firm in his principles, and undoubtedly one of the best politicians in America. Mr. Mason is about 60 years old, with a fine strong constitution.

Mr. Maddison is a character who has long been in public life; and what is very remarkable every Person seems to acknowledge his greatness. He blends together the profound politician, with the Scholar. In the management of every great question he evidently took the lead in the Convention, and tho' he cannot be called an Orator, he is a most agreable, eloquent, and convincing Speaker. From a spirit of industry and application which he possesses in a most eminent degree, he always comes forward the best informed Man of any point in debate. The affairs of the United States, he perhaps, has the most correct knowledge of, of any Man in the Union. He has been twice a Member of Congress, and was always thought one of the ablest Members that ever sat in that Council. Mr. Maddison is about 37 years of age, a Gentleman of great modesty,—with a remarkable sweet temper. He is easy and unreserved among his acquaintance, and has a most agreable style of conversation.

. . . Mr. Randolph is Governor of Virginia,—a young Gentleman in whom united all the accomplishments of the Scholar, and the States-man. He came forward with the postulata, or first principles, on which the Convention acted, and he supported them with a force of eloquence and reasoning that did him great honor. He has a most harmonious voice, a fine person and striking manners. Mr. Randolph is about 32 years of age. . . .

Mr. Davey is a Lawyer of some eminence in his State. He is said to have a good classical education, and is a Gentleman of considerable literary talents. He was silent in the Convention, but his opinion was always respected. Mr. Davey is about 30 years of age.

. . . Mr. Rutledge is one of those characters who was highly mounted at the commencement of the late revolution;—his reputation in the first Congress gave him a distinguished rank among the American Worthies. . . . Mr. Rutledge was once Governor of South Carolina. He is about 48 years of age. . . .

Mr. Charles Pinckney is a young Gentleman of the most promising talents. He is, altho' only 24 ys. of age, in possession of a very great variety of knowledge. Government, Law, History and Phylosophy are his favorite studies, but he is intimately acquainted with every species of polite learning, and has a spirit of application and industry beyond most Men. . . .

Mr. Baldwin is a Gentleman of superior abilities, and joins in a public debate with great art and eloquence. Having laid the foundation of a compleat classical education at Harvard College, he pursues every other study with ease. He is well acquainted with Books and Characters, and has an accomodating turn of mind, which enables him to gain the confidence of Men, and to understand them. He is a practising Attorney in Georgia, and has been twice a Member of Congress. Mr. Baldwin is about 38 years of age.

Mr. Houstoun is an Attorney at Law, and has been a Member of Congress for the State of Georgia. He is a Gentleman of Family, and was educated in England. As to his legal or political knowledge he has very little to boast of. Nature seems to have done more for his corporeal than mental powers. His Person is striking, but his mind very little improved with useful or elegant knowledge. He has none of the talents requisite for the Orator, but in public debate is confused and irregular. Mr. Houstoun is about 30 years of age of an amiable and sweet temper, and of good and honorable principles.

My own character I shall not attempt to draw, but leave those who may choose to speculate on it, to consider it in any light that their fancy or imagination may depict. I am conscious of having discharged my duty as a Soldier through the course of the late revolution with honor and propriety; and my services in congress and the Convention were bestowed with the best intention towards the interest of Georgia, and towards the general welfare of the Confederacy. I possess ambition, and it was that, and the flattering opinion which some of my Friends had of me, that gave me a seat in the wisest Council in the World, and furnished me with an opportunity of giving these short Sketches of the Characters who composed it.

The Virginia Plan

The Convention was scheduled to begin on the second Monday in May, 1787. A wet spring that year left the roads muddy and impassable, however, resulting in many delegates arriving late.

The proceedings finally began in late May, with a quorum of seven states present. The Virginia delegates came prepared with fifteen resolutions, later named the Virginia Plan, which became the basis for a new constitution.

James Madison was the author of these resolutions, although it was Virginia Governor Edmund Randolph who presented them to the Convention. Madison also kept detailed notes of each day's proceedings. What follows are his notes from Tuesday, May 29.

(From *Documentary History of the Constitution of the United States of America, 1786-1870.* Washington, DC: Department of State, 1900)

Mr. Randolph opened the main business.

He expressed his regret, that it should fall to him, rather than those, who were of longer standing in life and political experience, to open the great subject of their mission. But, as the convention had originated from Virginia, and his colleagues supposed that some proposition was expected from them, they had imposed this task on him.

He then commented on the difficulty of the crisis, and the necessity of preventing the fulfilment of the prophecies of the American downfall.

He observed that in revising the federal system we ought to inquire 1. into the properties which such a government ought to possess, 2. the defects of the confederation, 3. the danger of our situation, & 4. the remedy.

1. The character of such a government ought to secure 1) against foreign invasion; 2) against dissentions between members of the Union, or seditions in particular states; 3) to procure to the several states various blessings, of which an isolated situation was incapable; 4) to be able to defend itself against incroachment; & 5) to be paramount to the state constitutions.

2. In speaking of the defects of the confederation he professed a high respect for its authors, and considered them as having done all that patriots could do, in the then infancy of the science of constitutions & of confederacies,—when the inefficiency of requisitions was unknown—no commercial discord had arisen among any states—no rebellion had appeared as in Massts.*—foreign debts had not become urgent —the havoc of paper money had not been fore-seen— treaties had not been violated—and perhaps nothing better could be obtained from the jealousy of the states with regard to their sovereignty.

He then proceeded to enumerate the defects: 1) that the confederation produced no security against foreign invasion; congress not being permitted to prevent a war nor to support it by their own authority —Of this he cited many examples; most of which tended to shew that they could not cause infractions of treaties or of the law of nations to be punished: that particular states might by their conduct provoke war without controul; and that neither militia nor draughts being fit for defence on such occasions, enlistments only could be successful, and these could not be executed without money; 2) that the federal government could not check the quarrels between states, nor a rebellion in any, not having constitutional power nor means to interpose according to the exigency; 3) that there were many advantages, which the U.S. might acquire, which were not attainable under the confederation—such as a productive impost—counteraction of the commercial regulations of other nations—pushing of commerce ad libitum—&c &c. 4) that the federal government could not defend itself against the incroachments from the states; 5) that it was not even paramount to the state constitutions, ratified as it was in many of the states.

3. He next reviewed the danger of our situation [and] appealed to the sense of the best friends of the U.S.—the prospect of anarchy from the laxity of government everywhere; and to other considerations.

4. He then proceeded to the remedy; the basis of which he said, must be the republican principle.

He proposed as conformable to his ideas the following resolutions, which he explained one by one.

Resolutions proposed by Mr. Randolph in Convention (May 29, 1787)

I. *Resolved,* that the Articles of Confederation* ought to be so corrected and enlarged as to accomplish the objects proposed by their institution; namely, 'common defence, security of liberty and general welfare.'

2. *Resolved therefore,* that the rights of suffrage in the National Legislature ought to be proportioned to the quotas of contribution, or to the number of free inhabitants, as the one or the other rule may seem best in different cases.

3. *Resolved,* that the National Legislature ought to consist of two branches.

4. *Resolved*, that the members of the first branch of the National Legislature ought to be elected by the people of the several States every   for the term of   ; to be of the age of   years at least, to receive liberal stipends by which they may be compensated for the devotion of their time to the public service; to be ineligible to any office established by a particular State, or under the authority of the United States, except those peculiarly belonging to the functions of the first branch, during the term of service, and for the space of   after its expiration; to be incapable of re-election for the space of   after the expiration of their term of service, and to be subject to recall.

5. *Resolved*, that the members of the second branch of the National Legislature ought to be elected by those of the first, out of a proper number of persons nominated by the individual Legislatures, to be of the age of   years at least; to hold their offices for a term sufficient to ensure their independence; to receive liberal stipends, by which they may be compensated for the devotion of their time to the public service; and to be ineligible to any office established by a particular State, or under the authority of the United States, except those peculiarly belonging to the functions of the second branch, during the term of service, and for the space of   after the expiration thereof.

6. *Resolved*, that each branch ought to possess the right of originating Acts; that the National Legislature ought to be impowered to enjoy the legislative rights vested in Congress by the Confederation, and moreover to legislate in all cases to which the separate States are incompetent, or in which the harmony of the United States may be interrupted by the exercise of individual legislation; to negative all laws passed by the several States, contravening, in the opinion of the National Legislature the articles of Union; and to call forth the force of the Union

against any member of the Union failing to fulfil its duty under the articles thereof.

7. *Resolved*, that a National Executive be instituted; to be chosen by the National Legislature for the term of years, to receive punctually at stated times, a fixed compensation for the services rendered, in which no increase nor diminution shall be made so as to affect the magistracy, existing at the time of increase or diminution, and to be ineligible a second time; and that besides a general authority to execute the national laws, it ought to enjoy the executive rights vested in Congress by the Confederation.

8. *Resolved*, that the Executive and a convenient number of the National Judiciary, ought to compose a Council of Revision with authority to examine every Act of the National Legislature before it shall operate, and every Act of a particular Legislature before a negative thereon shall be final; and that the dissent of the said Council shall amount to a rejection, unless the Act of the national Legislature be again passed, or that of a particular Legislature be again negatived by of the members of each branch.

9. *Resolved*, that a National Judiciary be established to consist of one or more supreme tribunals, and of inferior tribunals to be chosen by the National Legislature, to hold their offices during good behaviour; and to receive punctually at stated times fixed compensation for their services, in which no increase or diminution shall be made so as to affect the persons actually in office at the time of such increase or diminution. That the jurisdiction of the inferior tribunals shall be to hear and determine in the first instance, and of the supreme tribunal to hear and determine in the dernier [last] resort, all piracies and felonies on the high seas, captures from an enemy, cases in which foreigners or citizens of other States applying to such jurisdictions may be interested, or

which respect the collection of the national revenue; impeachments of any National officers, and questions which may involve the national peace and harmony.

10. *Resolved*, that provision ought to be made for the admission of States lawfully arising within the limits of the United States, whether from a voluntary junction of government and territory or otherwise, with the consent of a number of voices in the National Legislature less than the whole.

11. *Resolved*, that a republican government and the territory of each State, except in the instance of a voluntary junction of Government and territory, ought to be guarantied by the United States to each State.

12. *Resolved*, that provision ought to be made for the continuance of Congress and their authorities and privileges, until a given day after the reform of the articles of Union shall be adopted, and for the completion of all their engagements.

13. *Resolved*, that provision ought to be made for the amendment of the Articles of Union whensoever it shall seem necessary, and that the assent of the National Legislature ought not to be required thereto.

14. *Resolved*, that the legislative, executive and judiciary powers within the several States ought to be bound by oath to support the articles of Union.

15. *Resolved*, that the amendments which shall be offered to the Confederation by the Convention, ought at a proper time or times, after the approbation of Congress, to be submitted to an assembly or assemblies of representatives recommended by the several Legislatures to be expressly chosen by the people, to consider and decide thereon.

He concluded with an exhortation, not to suffer the present opportunity of establishing general peace, harmony, happiness and liberty in the United States to pass away unimproved.

It was then *resolved*—That the House will tomorrow resolve itself into a committee of the whole house to consider of the state of the American Union, and that the propositions moved by Mr. Randolph be referred to the said committee.

Designing the Executive Department

The states chose seventy-four delegates to attend the Federal Convention, though only fifty-five actually attended. No matter how many delegates a state had, when it came time to vote on an issue, it was one state/one vote. A majority vote decided each issue.

The delegates also decided early on to keep the proceedings secret. (Madison's comprehensive notes on the proceedings were not published until 1840, more than fifty years later.) This encouraged a freer debate: allowing delegates to reopen discussions, change their minds, explore options, take another vote on important issues.

Madison's notes for June 1 record the delegates' discussion of Resolution 7 in the Virginia Plan—the establishment of a national executive.

(From *Sources and Documents Illustrating the American Revolution and the Formation of the Federal Constitution, 1764-1788.* S.E. Morrison, ed. London: Oxford University Press, 1923)

MR. PINCKNEY [S.C.] was for a vigorous Executive but was afraid the executive powers of the existing Congress might extend to peace and war, etc., which would render the Executive a monarchy of the worst kind, to wit, an elective one.

MR. WILSON [Pa.] moved that the Executive consist of a single person. MR. C. PINCKNEY seconded the motion, so as to read 'that a National Executive, to consist of a single person, be instituted.'

A considerable pause ensuing, and the chairman asking if he should put the question, DR. FRANKLIN

[Pa.] observed that it was a point of great importance, and wished that the gentlemen would deliver their sentiments on it before the question was put.

MR. RUTLEDGE [S.C.] animadverted on the shyness of gentlemen on this and other subjects. He said it looked as if they supposed themselves precluded by having frankly disclosed their opinions from afterwards changing them, which he did not take to be at all the case. He said he was for vesting the Executive Power in a single person, tho' he was not for giving him the power of war and peace. A single man would feel the greatest responsibility and administer the public affairs best.

MR. SHERMAN [Conn.] said he considered the executive magistracy as nothing more than an institution for carrying the will of the Legislature into effect, that the person or persons ought to be appointed by and accountable to the Legislature only, which was the depositary of the supreme will of the society. As they were the best judges of the business which ought to be done by the executive department, and consequently of the number necessary from time to time for doing it, he wished the number might not be fixed, but that the legislature should be at liberty to appoint one or more as experience might dictate.

MR. WILSON [Pa.] preferred a single magistrate, as giving most energy, dispatch, and responsibility to the office. He did not consider the prerogatives of the British monarch as a proper guide in defining the executive powers. Some of these prerogatives were of a legislative nature. Among others, that of war and peace, etc. The only powers he considered strictly executive were those of executing the laws and appointing officers, not appertaining to and appointed by the Legislature.

The Philadelphia State House, also known as Independence Hall, where the Federal Convention met during the summer of 1787.

MR. GERRY [Mass.] favored the policy of annexing a Council to the executive, in order to give weight and inspire confidence.

MR. RANDOLPH [Va.] strenuously opposed a unity in the executive magistracy. He regarded it as the fetus of monarchy. We had he said no motive to be governed by the British government as our prototype. He did not mean, however, to throw censure on that excellent fabric. If we were in a situation to copy it, he did not know that he should be opposed to it; but the fixed genius of the people of America required a different form of government. He could not see why the great requisites for the executive department, vigor, despatch, and responsibility, could not be found in three men, as well as in one man. The Executive ought to be independent. It ought, therefore, in order to support its independence to consist of more than one.

MR. WILSON [Pa.] said that unity in the Executive, instead of being the fetus of monarch, would be the best safeguard against tyranny. He repeated that he was not governed by the British model, which was inapplicable to the situation of this country; the extent of which was so great, and the manners so republican, that nothing but a great confederated republic would do for it.

Mr. Wilson's motion for a single magistrate was postponed by common consent, the committee seeming unprepared for any decision on it; and the first part of the clause agreed to, viz., 'that a National Executive be instituted.'

MR. MADISON [Va.] thought it would be proper, before a choice should be made between a unity and a plurality in the Executive, to fix the extent of the executive authority; that as certain powers were in their nature executive, and must be given to that department whether administered by one or more persons, a definition of their extent would assist the judgment in determining how far they might be safely entrusted to a single officer. He accordingly moved that so much of the clause before the committee as related to the powers of the Executive should be struck out, and that after the words 'that a National Executive ought to be instituted' there be inserted the words following, viz., 'with power to carry into effect the national laws, to appoint to offices in cases not otherwise provided for, and to execute such other powers not Legislative nor Judiciary in their nature, as may from time to time be delegated by the national Legislature.' . . .

The next clause in Resolution 7, relating to the mode of appointing, and the duration of, the Executive, being under consideration.

MR. WILSON [Pa.] said he was almost unwilling to declare the mode which he wished to take place, being apprehensive that it might appear chimerical. He would say, however, at least that in theory he was for an election by the people. Experience, particularly in New York and Massachusetts, shewed that an election of the first magistrate by the people at large, was both a convenient and successful mode. The objects of choice in such cases must be persons whose merits have general notoriety.

MR. SHERMAN [Conn.] was for the appointment by the Legislature, and for making him absolutely dependent on that body, as it was the will of that which was to be executed. An independence of the Executive on the Supreme Legislature, was in his opinion the very essence of tyranny, if there was any such thing.

MR. WILSON [Pa.] moves that the blank for the term of duration should be filled with three years, observing at the same time that he preferred this short period, on the supposition that a re-eligibility would be provided for.

MR. PINCKNEY [S.C.] moves for seven years.

MR. SHERMAN [Conn.] was for three years, and against the doctrine of rotation, as throwing out of office the men best qualified to execute its duties.

MR. MASON [Va.] was for seven years at least, and for prohibiting a re-eligibility as the best expedient both for preventing the effect of a false complaisance on the side of the Legislature towards unfit characters; and a temptation on the side of the Executive to intrigue with the Legislature for a re-appointment.

MR. BEDFORD [Del.] was strongly opposed to so long a term as seven years. He begged the committee to consider that the situation of the country would be, in case the first magistrate should be saddled on it for such a period and it should be found on trial that he did not possess the qualifications ascribed to him, or should lose them after his appointment. An impeachment he said would be no cure for this evil, as an impeachment would reach misfeasance only, not incapacity. He was for a triennial election, and for an ineligibility after a period of nine years.

On the question for seven years,

Mass. divided. Conn. no. N.Y. ay. N.J. ay. Penn. ay. Del. ay. Va. ay. N.C. no. S.C. no. Geo. no. There being 5 ays, 4 noes, I divided,* a question was asked whether a majority had voted in the affirmative? The President decided that it was an affirmative vote.

By September, the delegates decided that a single person should hold executive power, and that the elected term of office would be four years.

Small States Oppose the Virginia Plan

Smaller states, such as New Jersey and Maryland, felt the Virginia Plan unfairly favored the large states at the expense of the small ones. On June 15, William Paterson [N.J.] put forth an alternate plan, which became known as the New Jersey Plan.

To clarify the debate, James Wilson [Pa.] summarized the differences between the Virginia and the New Jersey Plans this way:

(From *Documents Illustrative of the Formation of the Union of the AmericanStates.* Charles C. Tansill, ed. Washington, DC: Government Printing Office, 1927)

Virginia Plan proposes two branches in the legislature.

Jersey, a single legislative body.

Virginia, the legislative powers derived from the people.

Jersey, from the states.

Virginia, a single executive.

Jersey, more than one.

Virginia, a majority of the legislature can act.

Jersey, a small minority can control.

Virginia, the legislature can legislate on all national concerns.

Jersey, only on limited objects.

Virginia, legislature to negative all state laws.

Jersey, giving power to the executive to compel obedience by force.

Virginia, to remove the executive by impeachment.

Jersey, on application of a majority of the states.

Virginia, for the establishment of inferior judiciary tribunals.

Jersey, no provision.

One of the most vocal opponents of the Virginia Plan was Maryland delegate (and attorney general of that state) Luther Martin. Martin was rather long-winded, which, on the hottest days during that long summer of 1787, did not make him particularly popular. In his June 27 speech before the Convention, Martin finds fault with the Virginia Plan, and questions the authority of the delegates to do anything more than amend the Articles of Confederation. Martin's speech, excerpted below, was recorded in the notes of New York delegate Robert Yates.

Unequal confederacies can never produce good effects. Apply this to the Virginia Plan. Out of the number 90, Virginia has 16 votes, Massachusetts 14, Pennsylvania 12—in all 42. Add to this a state having four votes, and it gives a majority in the general legislature. Consequently a combination of these states will govern the remaining nine or ten states. Where is the safety and independency of those states? Pursue this subject farther. The executive is to be appointed by the legislature, and becomes the executive in consequence of this undue influence. And hence flows the appointment of all your officers, civil, military, and judicial. The executive is also to have a negative on all laws. Suppose the possibility of a combination of ten states; he negatives a law; it is totally lost, because those states cannot form two-thirds of the legislature. I am willing to give up private interest for the public good, but I must be satisfied first that it is the public interest. Who can decide this point? A majority only of the union. . . .

I would rather confederate with any single state, than submit to the Virginia Plan. But we are already confederated, and no power on earth can dissolve it but by the consent of *all* the contracting powers, and four states, on this floor, have already declared their opposition to annihilate it. Is the old confederation dissolved because some of the states wish a new confederation?

The New Jersey Plan was voted down on June 19, but it took another month of debate before the large and small states reached an agreement concerning representation in the legislature. The Great Compromise, adopted by the Convention on July 16, called for proportional representation (based on a state's population) in the House, and equal representation (two votes per state, whether large or small) in the Senate.*

The Signing

The Great Compromise proved to be a turning point. By July 26, the Convention adjourned for eleven days to allow a Committee of Detail (Randolph, Wilson, Rutledge, Gorham, and Ellsworth) to draft a Report of the resolutions and ideas agreed to so far. Five more weeks of intensive debate followed, in which the delegates discussed the Report and hammered out decisions about commerce, elections, and the slave trade.

From September 8-10, the Committee of Style (Johnson, Hamilton, Madison, King, and Gouverneur Morris) arranged the agreed-upon proposals into a Constitution consisting of seven articles. Gouverneur Morris also rewrote the Preamble: from "We the undersigned delegates of the States of New Hampshire, Massachusetts-bay . . ." to "We the People of the United States . . ."

On September 12, the proposal of George Mason [Va.] for adding a bill of rights to the Constitution was defeated: every state voted against it. The Convention approved the Constitution on Saturday, September 15, and ordered the final copy to be written out on parchment.

The closing day of the Convention was Monday, September 17, 1787: the day the delegates gathered in Philadelphia's Independence Hall to sign the Constitution. Madison's notes for that day include the following speech by Benjamin Franklin.

(From *Documents Illustrative of the Formation of the Union of the American States*. Charles C. Tansill, ed. Washington, DC: Government Printing Office, 1927; also from *The Records of the Federal Convention of 1787*. Max Farrand, ed. CT: Yale University Press, 1911)

Dr. Franklin [Pa.] rose with a speech in his hand, which he had reduced to writing for his own convenience, and which Mr. Wilson read in the words following:

Mr. President,

I confess that there are several parts of this constitution which I do not at present approve, but I am not sure that I shall never approve them: For, having lived long, I have experienced many instances of being obliged by better information or fuller consideration to change opinions even on important subjects, which I once thought right, but found to be otherwise. It is therefore that the older I grow, the more apt I am to doubt my own judgment, and to pay more respect to the judgment of others. Most men indeed as well as most sects in Religion, think themselves in the possession of all truth and that wherever others differ from them it is so far error . . .

In these sentiments, Sir, I agree to this Constitution with all its faults, if they are such, because I think a general Government necessary for us and there is no form of Government but what may be a blessing to the people if well administered, and believe farther that this is likely to be well administered for a course of years, and can only end in Despotism, as other forms have done before it, when the people have become so corrupted as to need despotic Government, being incapable of any other. I doubt too whether any other Convention we can obtain may be able to make a better Constitution.

The Signing of the Constitution, with George Washington presiding (painting by H.C. Christy)

For when you assemble a number of men to have the advantage of their joint wisdom, you inevitably assemble with those men, all their prejudices, their passions, their errors of opinion, their local interests, and their selfishness. From such an Assembly can a perfect production be expected? It therefore astonishes me, Sir, to find this system approaching so near to perfection as it does and I think it will astonish our enemies, who are waiting with confidence to hear that our councils are confounded like those of the Builders of Babel; and that our States are on the point of separation, only to meet hereafter for the purpose of cutting one another's throats. Thus I consent, Sir, to this Constitution because I expect no better, and because I am not sure it is not the best. The opinions I have had of its errors, I sacrifice to the public good—I have never whispered a syllable of them abroad—Within these walls they were born, and here they shall die—If every one of us in returning to our Constituents were to report the objections he has had to it, and endeavor to gain partizans in support of them, we might prevent its being generally received, and thereby lose all the salutary effects & great advantages resulting naturally in our favor among foreign Nations as well as among ourselves, from our real or apparent unanimity. Much of the strength & efficiency of any Government in procuring and securing happiness to the people, depends on opinion, on the general opinion of the goodness of the Government, as well as of the wisdom and integrity of its Governors. I hope therefore that for our own sakes as a part of the people, and for the sake of posterity, we shall act heartily and unanimously in recommending this Constitution (if approved by Congress & confirmed by the Conventions) wherever our influence may extend, and turn our future thoughts & endeavors to the means of having it well administered.

On the whole, Sir, I cannot help expressing a wish that every member of the Convention who may still have objections to it, would with me, on this occasion doubt a little of his own infallibility—and to make manifest our unanimity, put his name to this instrument.

While the last members were signing it, Dr. Franklin, looking toward the President's chair, at the back of which a rising sun happened to be painted, observed to a few members near him, that painters had found it difficult to distinguish in their art a rising from a setting sun. "I have," said he, "often, and often in the course of the session, and the vicissitudes of my hopes and fears as to its issue, looked at that behind the President without being able to tell whether it was rising or setting. But now at length I have the happiness to know that it is a rising and not a setting sun."

Thirty-nine of the forty-two delegates present on September 17, 1787, signed the official copy of the Constitution. The Convention then adjourned for the final time.

It's Up to the States

The Continental Congress received the proposed Constitution on September 20, 1787, while meeting in New York City (where the Capitol was at that time). After a week's debate, they resolved to submit the Constitution to the states for ratification. Pennsylvania was one of the first states to call a special ratifying convention.

James Wilson Addressing the Pennsylvania Convention (December 3, 1787)

(From *Pennsylvania and the Federal Constitution*, McMaster and Stone, ed. New York: De Capo Press, 1970. Originally published in 1888)

Much fault has been found with the mode of expression used in the first clause of the ninth section of the first article.* I believe I can assign a reason why that mode of expression was used, and why the term slave was not directly admitted in this constitution . . .

Under the present confederation, the States may admit the importation of slaves as long as they please; but by this article, after the year 1808, the Congress will have power to prohibit such importation, notwithstanding the disposition of any State to the contrary. I consider this as laying the foundation for banishing slavery out of this country; and though the period is more distant than I could wish, yet it will produce the same kind, gradual change which was pursued in Pennsylvania. . . .

But an immediate advantage is also obtained, for a tax or duty may be imposed on such importation not exceeding ten dollars for each person; and this, Sir, operates as a partial prohibition. It was all that could be obtained. I am sorry it was not more; but from this I think there is reason to hope that yet a few years, and it will be prohibited altogether. And in the meantime, the new States which are to be formed will be under the control of Congress in this particular, and slaves will never be introduced amongst them. The gentleman says that it is unfortunate in another point of view: it means to prohibit the introduction of white people from Europe, as this tax may deter them from coming amongst us. A little impartiality and attention will discover the care that the convention took in selecting their language. The words are, the *migration* or IMPORTATION of such persons, etc., shall not be prohibited by Congress prior to the year 1808, but a tax or duty may be imposed on such IMPORTATION. It is observable here that the term migration is dropped when a tax or duty is mentioned, so that Congress [will] have power to impose the tax only on those imported.

Nine states needed to ratify the Constitution in order for it to go into effect. Delaware was the first state to ratify: with a unanimous vote on December 7, 1787. The Pennsylvania and New Jersey conventions also ratified in December. Other states followed suit in early 1788: Georgia and Connecticut (January), Massachusetts (February), Maryland (April), and South Carolina (May).

The ninth state to ratify the Constitution was New Hampshire, on June 21, 1788. The conventions in two of the largest states—Virginia and New York—ratified in June and July, 1788, respectively. North

Carolina and Rhode Island held off ratifying the Constitution until after the new government was established.

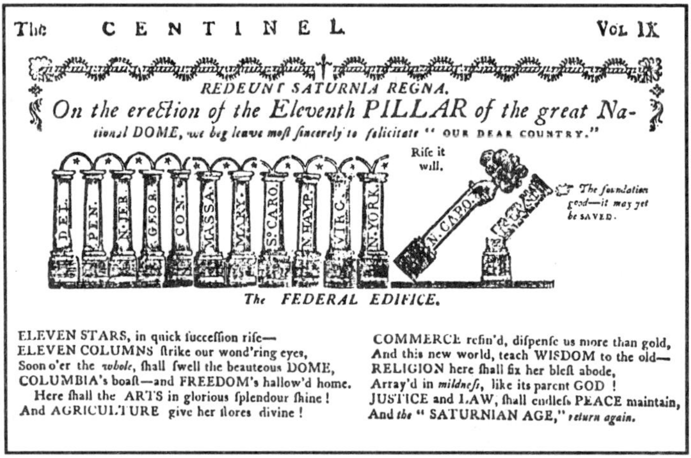
The CENTINEL. Vol. IX

REDEUNT SATURNIA REGNA.

On the erection of the Eleventh PILLAR of the great National DOME, we beg leave moſt ſincerely to felicitate " OUR DEAR COUNTRY."

The FEDERAL EDIFICE.

ELEVEN STARS, in quick ſucceſſion riſe—
ELEVEN COLUMNS ſtrike our wond'ring eyes,
Soon o'er the *whole*, ſhall ſwell the beauteous DOME,
COLUMBIA's boaſt—and FREEDOM's hallow'd home.
Here ſhall the ARTS in glorious ſplendour ſhine!
And AGRICULTURE give her ſtores divine!

COMMERCE refin'd, diſpenſe us more than gold,
And this new world, teach WISDOM to the old—
RELIGION here ſhall fix her bleſt abode,
Array'd in *mildneſs*, like its parent GOD!
JUSTICE and LAW, ſhall endleſs PEACE maintain,
And *the* "SATURNIAN AGE," *return again.*

The Massachusetts Centinel *on August 2, 1788 urged North Carolina and Rhode Island to ratify the Constitution to fortify the "Federal Ediface."*

First Among the Framers

James Madison,
"Father of the Constitution.

James Madison, the 5'4" delegate from Virginia, was once described as "no bigger than half a piece of soap." His voice was so quiet that other delegates frequently asked him to speak louder in Convention. How did this small, quiet man become known as the "Father of the Constitution"?

One reason was the depth of his preparation. Well before the Convention began in May of 1787, Madison was busy studying confederacies and constitutions. His knowledge of political theory extended from classical to Western European governments, and from ancient to modern times. At one point, Madison wrote a lengthy comparison of governments, concluding with a section of his own titled "Vices of the Political System of the United States."

Madison was also the author of the Virginia Plan: the resolutions, presented by Randolph on May 29, which set the agenda for the Convention. In a letter to George Washington in April, Madison had listed the major issues the Convention would need to address. The Virginia delegation's prompt arrival in Philadelphia gave them time to further discuss and prepare the Plan, before the others arrived and the Convention got under way.

Madison saw the need for a strong national government, based on the *people* rather than on the states. During the Convention, he repeatedly nudged his colleagues back toward this line of thinking. The delegates had gathered in Philadelphia to amend the Articles of Confederation; yet within the first week of the Convention, they found themselves discussing the Virginia Plan as the frame for a new constitution. Months later, on the issue of whether the people or the state legislatures should ratify the proposed constitution, Madison told them: "I consider the difference between a system founded on the legislatures only, and one founded on the people, to be the true difference between a league or treaty and a *constitution.*"

Throughout the Convention, the 36-year-old Madison's participation was intense yet courteous. He pursued issues logically, and above all, was well-informed. When the fears of the smaller states threatened to stall debate in mid-June, Madison calmly detailed, point by point, the problems with the New Jersey Plan they favored. Madison's June 19 speech reassured the delegates of both small and large states, providing damage control from Hamilton's extremely nationalist speech* of the day before. By day's end, the vote was seven states to three to use the Virginia Plan as a basis for debate, effectively killing the New Jersey Plan.

In all, Madison gave 161 speeches during the Convention on issues great and small. He offered ideas and suggestions to fellow delegates searching for solutions and points of compromise. He served on key committees, including the Committee on Postponed Matters (filling in the details of adopted resolutions) and the Committee of Style (producing the final draft of the Constitution).

Remarkably, in addition to such active participation, Madison kept detailed notes of the entire Convention proceedings. He later explained:

> I chose a seat in front of the presiding member [Washington] with the other members, on my right & left hand. In this favorable position for hearing all that passed, I noted in terms legible & in abbreviations & marks intelligible to myself what was read from the Chair or spoken by the members; and losing not a moment unnecessarily between the adjournment & reassembling of the Convention I was enabled to write out my daily notes during the session or within a few finishing days after its close . . .

It was a lucky break for history: the man who'd been paid to keep such a record, Major Jackson of South Carolina, kept a sketchy journal at best. Madison's notes have provided us with the inside, day-by-day view of the debates we have today.

Madison recognized, however, that the Convention's work was only the first step. The proposed Constitution needed to be reviewed by the Continental Congress, ratified by the people, and then put into practice by a newly established government. Madison continued to play a key role each step along the way.

Once the Constitution was signed, Madison returned to the Continental Congress in New York to begin plans for the ratification campaign. Congress passed the Constitution on to the states for ratification by the end of September. Public debate heated up at once: Where was the protection of individual rights? Should the states relinquish so much to the national government?

In New York, Alexander Hamilton began a series of newspaper articles, signed Publius, setting out the arguments in favor of the Constitution. Madison joined him in this work, as did John Jay, and their combined efforts produced 85 essays which appeared initially in the *New York Independent Journal* between October, 1787, and April, 1788. The essays were reprinted in newspapers in various states, became popular as a debater's handbook in the state ratifying conventions, and later came out in book form as *The Federalist Papers.*

The Federalist No. 10, written by Madison, is perhaps the most famous of these essays. It addressed the problem of "factions"—local majorities gaining control and creating bad law by acting purely on self-interest. Madison argued that factions would lack such opportunity for control under the Constitution,

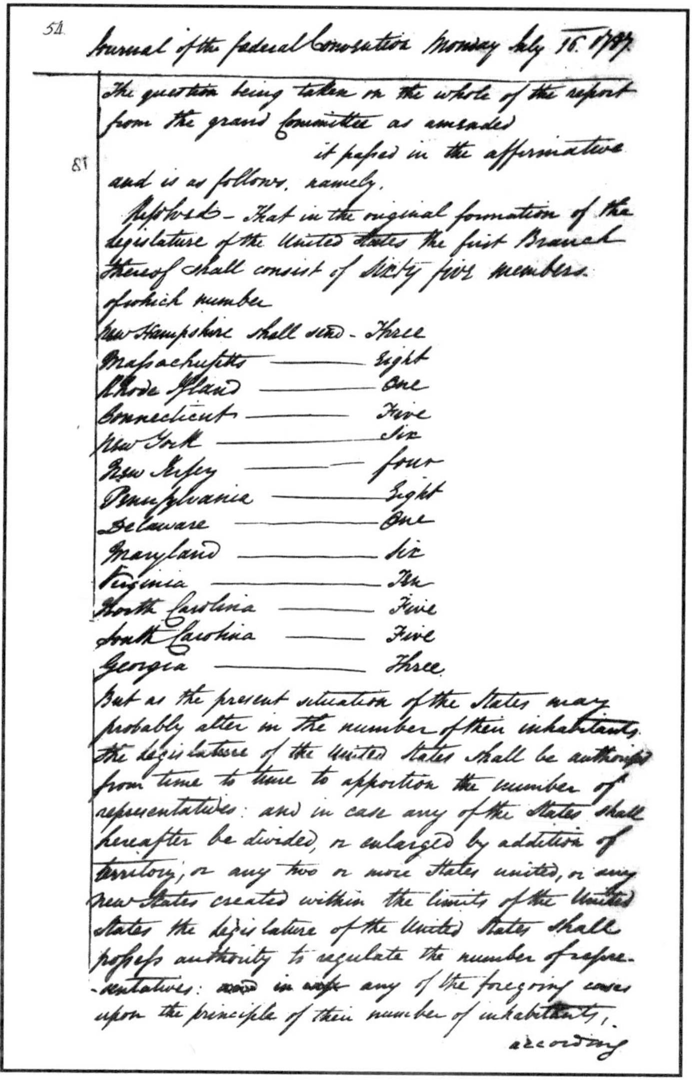
54 Journal of the federal Convention Monday July 16. 1787

The question being taken on the whole of the report from the grand Committee as amended

it passed in the affirmative

81 and is as follows, namely.

Resolved - That in the original formation of the Legislature of the United States the first Branch thereof shall consist of sixty five members. of which number

New Hampshire shall send	Three
Massachusetts	Eight
Rhode Island	One
Connecticut	Five
New York	Six
New Jersey	four
Pennsylvania	Eight
Delaware	One
Maryland	Six
Virginia	Ten
North Carolina	Five
South Carolina	Five
Georgia	Three

But as the present situation of the States may probably alter in the number of their inhabitants, the legislature of the United States shall be authorized from time to time to apportion the number of representatives: and in case any of the States shall hereafter be divided, or enlarged by addition of territory, or any two or more States united, or any new States created within the limits of the United States the legislature of the United States shall possess authority to regulate the number of representatives: ~~and~~ in ~~case~~ any of the foregoing cases upon the principle of their number of inhabitants, according

This page from the convention journal records "The Great Compromise" in which states were to be represented in the House according to population.

which "extends the sphere" of government to cover a larger territory.

Back in Virginia in the spring of 1788, Madison was elected to his home state's ratifying convention. He put aside his own disappointments about certain parts of the Constitution and worked tirelessly to achieve the goal of ratification. The competition was stiff: Patrick Henry gave speech after fiery anti-federalist speech. Though the vote was close, 89 to 79, the Virginia Convention ratified the Constitution on June 25, 1788.

The battle was won; more than nine states had ratified the Constitution. Still, Madison did not rest. In 1789, as a member of the House of Representatives under the new Constitution, Madison sponsored a group of constitutional amendments. He based them largely on Virginia's Declaration of Rights. Twelve of the amendments passed Congress; ten of those were ratified by the states by the end of 1791. They are our Bill of Rights.

Madison went on to serve as the nation's Secretary of State for eight years, and in 1809, was elected as the fourth President of the United States. The small, quiet man from Virginia had proven himself to be the chief architect and bricklayer of our government's foundation: from framing the Constitution to sponsoring the Bill of Rights, and beyond.

Creating a National Bill of Rights

The major complaint in the states was that the proposed Constitution lacked a bill of rights. The conventions in several states, including Massachusetts and Virginia, submitted proposed amendments with their vote for ratification.

After all, the struggle with Great Britain for certain freedoms was still a fresh memory. Eight of the state constitutions included bills of rights.

George Mason wrote Virginia's Bill of Rights, reprinted below, which Madison turned to in drafting amendments for a U.S. Bill of Rights. You'll recognize a number of phrases and concepts here which later found their way into the Declaration of Independence (July 4, 1776) and the main body of the Constitution (September 17, 1787), as well as the U.S. Bill of Rights.

The Virginia Declaration of Rights
12 June 1776

(FROM *Statutes at Large of Virginia*, W.W. Hening, ed., 1821; also from *Sources and Documents Illustrating the American Revolution and the Formation of the Federal Constitution, 1764-1788.* S.E. Morrison, ed. London: Oxford University Press, 1923)

AT A GENERAL CONVENTION of Delegates and Representatives, from the several counties and corporations of Virginia, held at the Capitol in the City of Williamsburg on Monday the 6th May 1776.

George Mason,
author of the Virginia Bill of Rights

A declaration of Rights made by the representatives of the good people of Virginia, assembled in full and free Convention; which rights do pertain to them and their posterity, as the basis and foundation of government.

I. That all men are by nature equally free and independent, and have certain inherent rights, of which, when they enter into a state of society, they cannot by any compact deprive or divest their posterity; namely, the enjoyment of life and liberty, with the means of acquiring and possessing property, and pursuing and obtaining happiness and safety.

2. That all power is vested in, and consequently derived from, the people; that magistrates are their trustees and servants, and at all times amenable to them.

3. That government is, or ought to be instituted for the common benefit, protection, and security of the people, nation, or community; of all the various modes and forms of government, that is best which is capable of producing the greatest degree of happiness and safety, and is most effectually secured against the danger of maladministration; and that when any government shall be found inadequate or contrary to these purposes, a majority of the community hath an indubitable, unalienable and indefeasible right to reform, alter or abolish it, in such manner as shall be judged most conducive to the public weal.

4. That no man, or set of men, are entitled to exclusive or separate emoluments or privileges from the community, but in consideration of publick services; which, not being descendible, neither ought the offices of magistrate, legislator or judge to be hereditary.

5. That the legislative and executive powers of the state should be separate and distinct from the judiciary; and that the members of the two first may be restrained from oppression, by feeling and participating the burthens of the people, they should, at fixed periods, be reduced to a private station, return into that body from which they were originally taken, and the vacancies be supplied by frequent, certain, and regular elections, in which all, or any part of the former members to be again eligible or ineligible, as the laws shall direct.

6. That elections of members to serve as representatives of the people in assembly, ought to be free; and that all men having sufficient evidence of permanent common interest with, and attachment

to the community, have the right of suffrage, and cannot be taxed or deprived of their property for publick uses, without their own consent, or that of their representatives so elected, nor bound by any law to which they have not, in like manner, assented for the public good.

7. That all power of suspending laws, or the execution of laws, by any authority without consent of the representatives of the people, is injurious to their rights, and ought not to be exercised.

8. That in all capital or criminal prosecutions a man hath a right to demand the cause and nature of his accusation, to be confronted with the accusers and witnesses, to call for evidence in his favour, and to a speedy trial by an impartial jury of his vicinage, without whose unanimous consent he cannot be found guilty; nor can he be compelled to give evidence against himself; that no man be deprived of his liberty, except by the law of the land or the judgment of his peers.

9. That excessive bail ought not to be required, nor excessive fines imposed, nor cruel and unusual punishments inflicted.

10. That general warrants, whereby an officer or messenger may be commanded to search suspected places without evidence of a fact committed, or to seize any person or persons not named, or whose offence is not particularly described and supported by evidence, are grievous and oppressive, and ought not to be granted.

11. That in controversies respecting property, and in suits between man and man, the ancient trial by jury is preferable to any other, and ought to be held sacred.

12. That the freedom of the press is one of the great bulwarks of liberty, and can never be restrained but by despotick governments.

13. That a well-regulated militia, composed of the body of the people trained to arms, is the proper, natural and safe defence of a free state; that standing armies in time of peace should be avoided as dangerous to liberty; and that in all cases the military should be under strict subordination to, and governed by, the civil power.

14. That the people have a right to uniform government; and, therefore, that no government separate from, or independent of the government of Virginia, ought to be erected or established within the limits thereof.

15. That no free government, or the blessings of liberty, can be preserved to any people, but by a firm adherence to justice, moderation, temperance, frugality and virtue, and by frequent recurrence to fundamental principles.

16. That religion, or the duty which we owe to our Creator, and the manner of discharging it, can be directed only by reason and conviction, not by force or violence; and therefore all men are equally entitled to the free exercise of religion, according to the dictates of conscience; and that it is the mutual duty of all to practise Christian forbearance, love, and charity towards each other.

Did You Know . . . ?

(From various sources, including *The Bill of Rights and Beyond,* and *The Bill of Rights: 200 Years, 200 Facts,* listed in Suggested Readings at the end of this book)

... that Philadelphia was our nation's capital when the Bill of Rights—the first ten amendments to the Constitution—was ratified?

... that by the time the Bill of Rights was ratified (approved by three-fourths of the states) on December 15, 1791, there were 14 states? Vermont had joined the thirteen original states.

... that many of the ideas in our Bill of Rights came from the Magna Carta (1215), the English Bill of Rights (1689), and the Virginia Bill of Rights (1776)?

... that the House and Senate originally submitted 12 proposed amendments to the states in 1789 for ratification? The states didn't ratify the first two amendments, which required one representative in Congress for every 50,000 people, and allowed no salary increase for Congress members to take effect until after the next election. More than 200 years later, in 1992, the Congressional salary amendment was ratified, becoming the 27th Amendment to our Constitution.

... that Connecticut, Georgia, and Massachusetts did not ratify the Bill of Rights before it went into effect?

... that the Fourteenth Amendment, adopted in 1868, made many of the Bill of Rights applicable to the states?

... that the Bill of Rights applies not only to American citizens, but also to foreign residents, visitors, even illegal immigrants in this country?

... that the "right to privacy" is not specifically listed in the Bill of Rights? It is founded on what the Supreme Court called the "right to be left alone," based on rights in the Fourth Amendment (against unreasonable searches and seizures), the Fifth Amendment (against self-incrimination), and the Ninth Amendment (unenumerated rights).

... that at the Constitutional Convention, three delegates refused to sign the Constitution because it lacked a Bill of Rights? They were George Mason and Edmund Randolph of Virginia, and Elbridge Gerry of Massachusetts.

... that the First Amendment, which contains our most precious rights, is just one sentence long? It reads: "Congress shall make no law respecting an establishment of religion, or prohibiting the free exercise thereof; or abridging the freedom of speech, or of the press, or the right of the people peaceably to assemble, and to petition the Government for a redress of grievances."

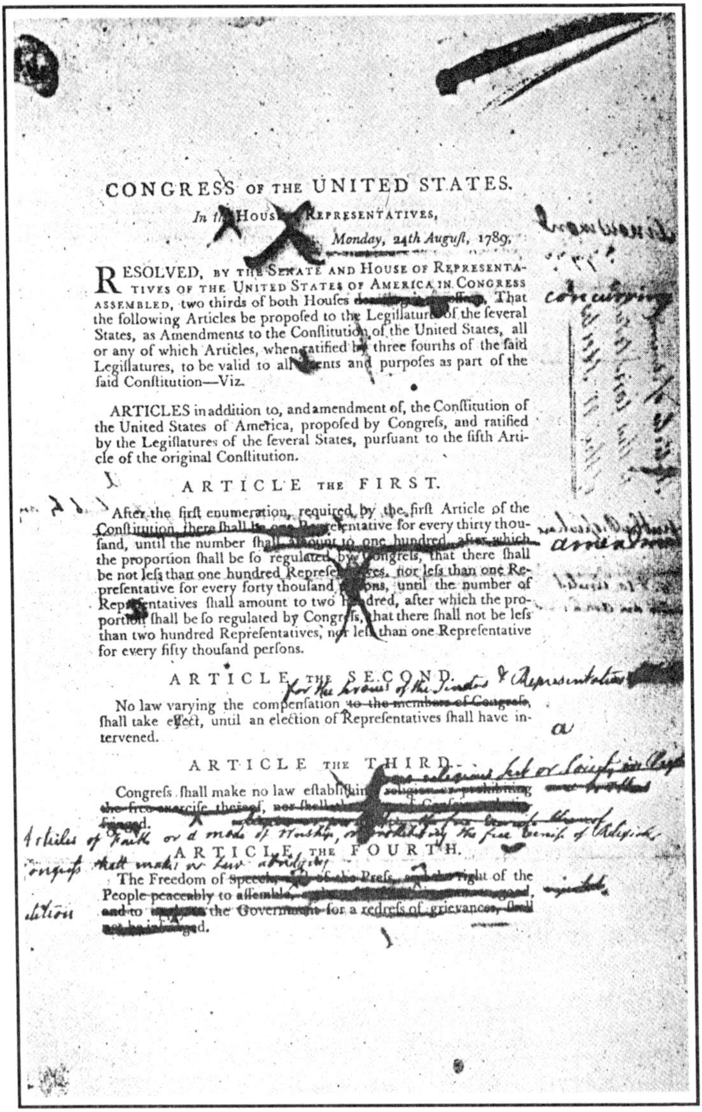
CONGRESS OF THE UNITED STATES.

In the House of Representatives,

Monday, 24th Auguſt, 1789.

RESOLVED, BY THE SENATE AND HOUSE OF REPRESENTATIVES OF THE UNITED STATES OF AMERICA IN CONGRESS ASSEMBLED, two thirds of both Houſes deeming it neceſſary, That the following Articles be propoſed to the Legiſlatures of the ſeveral States, as Amendments to the Conſtitution of the United States, all or any of which Articles, when ratified by three fourths of the ſaid Legiſlatures, to be valid to all intents and purpoſes as part of the ſaid Conſtitution—Viz.

ARTICLES in addition to, and amendment of, the Conſtitution of the United States of America, propoſed by Congreſs, and ratified by the Legiſlatures of the ſeveral States, purſuant to the fifth Article of the original Conſtitution.

ARTICLE THE FIRST.

After the firſt enumeration, required by the firſt Article of the Conſtitution, there ſhall be one Repreſentative for every thirty thouſand, until the number ſhall amount to one hundred, after which the proportion ſhall be ſo regulated by Congreſs, that there ſhall be not leſs than one hundred Repreſentatives, nor leſs than one Repreſentative for every forty thouſand perſons, until the number of Repreſentatives ſhall amount to two hundred, after which the proportion ſhall be ſo regulated by Congreſs, that there ſhall not be leſs than two hundred Repreſentatives, nor leſs than one Repreſentative for every fifty thouſand perſons.

ARTICLE THE SECOND.

No law varying the compenſation to the members of Congreſs, ſhall take effect, until an election of Repreſentatives ſhall have intervened.

ARTICLE THE THIRD.

Congreſs ſhall make no law eſtabliſhing religion or prohibiting the free exerciſe thereof, nor ſhall the rights of Conſcience be infringed.

ARTICLE THE FOURTH.

The Freedom of Speech, and of the Preſs, and the right of the People peaceably to aſſemble, and conſult for their common good, and to apply to the Government for a redreſs of grievances, ſhall not be infringed.

The first page of the Senate's working copy of the draft of the Bill of Rights, which became law in 1791.

Definitions

adjourn - to suspend proceedings to another time or place; to quit for the day

amend - to alter legislation formally by adding, deleting, or rephrasing

Bill of Rights - the first ten amendments to the U.S. Constitution, which protect more than thirty liberties and rights

confederation - a group of states that have united for a common purpose

constitution - the system of fundamental laws and principles that establishes the nature, functions, and limits of a government

delegate - an elected or appointed representative authorized to act on behalf of others

federal - the form of government in which power is divided between a central authority and a number of member units (such as states). Nowadays, the word "federal" is also used to refer to the central government in such a federation.

Federalist - those favoring a strong federal government; supporters of the proposed Constitution

quorum - the minimum number of members who must be present (usually a majority) to do valid business

ratify - to approve and so make valid

republican - the form of government in which the power lies with the citizens, who vote for officers and representatives responsible to them

resolution - a formal statement of a decision or expression of opinion put before or adopted by an assembly such as the U.S. Congress

resolve - to decide or express by formal vote

Notes

Continental Congress (p. 7): the assembly that declared and led the struggle for American Independence. Each of the 13 colonies (states after 1776) had one vote. The first Congress met for six weeks in 1774; the Second Continental Congress met initially in April 1775, and did not formally dissolve until replaced by the government under the present Constitution, adopted in 1788.

Shays' Rebellion (p. 16): In 1786, debt-ridden farmers in western Massachusetts protested foreclosures and heavy taxes by surrounding courthouses in various counties, to prevent foreclosure cases from being heard. (Daniel Shays led the 600 farmers who surrounded the Springfield courthouse.) As news spread to other states, fear of such civil disorder provided another reason to call for a federal convention.

Articles of Confederation (p. 17): The first constitution of the United States, adopted by the original 13 states in 1781 and lasting until 1788, when the present Constitution was ratified.

5 ays, 4 noes, I divided (p. 27): That only 10 states were represented in a vote was not unusual. Rhode Island had sent no delegates, and the New Hampshire delegates did not arrive until late July—a week after the Great Compromise was passed. On a typical day, no more than 30 delegates attended; most days, the group resembled a large committee.

a state's population (p. 30): The first federal census was not taken until 1790. The framers of the Constitution decided how many representatives each state could send to the House of Representatives until such a census was taken. *See* U.S. Constitution, Article 1, Section 2.

Article I, Section 9, Clause 1 (1787 Constitution) (p. 36): read "The Migration or Importation of such Persons as any of the States now existing shall think proper to admit, shall not be prohibited by the Congress prior to the Year one thousand eight hundred and eight, but a Tax or duty may be imposed on such Importation, not exceeding ten dollars for each Person."

Hamilton's nationalist speech (p. 41): Both Hamilton and Madison supported the Constitution and a strong national government. The difference was that Hamilton's radical words aroused his colleagues' fears; Madison's words worked toward compromise and consensus.

Suggestions for Further Reading

Note: Excerpts in this book from other sources are noted at the beginning of each reading.

Alderman, Ellen, and Caroline Kennedy. *In Our Defense: The Bill of Rights in Action.* New York: William Morrow and Co., Inc., 1991.

Atherton, Herbert, and J.J. Barlow, ed. *The Bill of Rights and Beyond.* Commission on the Bicentennial of the United States Constitution, 1990.

Bowen, Catherine Drinker. *Miracle of Philadelphia: The Story of the Constitutional Convention, May to September 1787.* Boston, MA: Little, Brown and Co., 1966.

Dudley, William, ed. *The Creation of the Constitution: Opposing Viewpoints.* San Diego, CA: Greenhaven Press, Inc., 1995.

Gardner, Joseph, ed. *James Madison, A Biography in His Own Words.* New York: Newsweek, Inc., 1974.

Hunt, Gaillard and J. B. Scott, ed. *The Debates in the Federal Convention of 1787.* Westport, CT: Greenwood Press, 1920.

Madison, James, and Alexander Hamilton, John Jay. *The Federalist Papers.* New York: New American Library, 1961 (one of many available editions; first published in 1787-88).

Morris, Richard B. *Witnesses at the Creation.* New York: Holt, Rinehart and Winston, 1985.

Rhodehamel, John. *Letters of Liberty*. Los Angeles, CA: Constituional Rights Foundation, 1988.

St. John, Jeffrey. *Constitutional Journal – A Correspondent's Report from the Convention of 1787.* Ottawa, IL: Jameson Books, Inc., 1987.

—— *Forge of Union– Anvil of Liberty*. Ottawa, IL: Jameson Books, Inc., 1992.

The Bill of Rights: 200 Years, 200 Facts. Philip Morris Mgmt. Corp., 1990.

Wright, Esmond. *Fabric of Freedom: 1763-1800.* New York: Hill and Wang, 1978.

Young, Alfred, and Terry Fife with Mary Janzen. *We the People – Voices and Images of the New Nation.* Philadelphia, PA: Temple University Press, 1993.

About the Editor

Ellen Hansen is a freelance writer. After graduating from Middlebury College (Vermont) and American University Law School (Washington, D.C.), she practiced law for a number of years, then taught German and English in Japan for three years.

This is her fifth book in the Perspectives on History Series for Discovery Enterprises.

Ms. Hansen lives with her husband in Portland, Oregon, and is currently at work on a book of essays and a biography of Nellie Bly.

The Perspectives on History Series

THE LOWELL MILL GIRLS: Life in the Factory

VOICES FROM THE WEST: Life Along the Trail

COMING TO AMERICA: A New Life in a New Land

FAITH UNFURLED: The Pilgrims' Quest for Freedom

THE NEW ENGLAND TRANSCENDENTALISTS: Life of the Mind and of the Spirit

FORWARD INTO LIGHT: The Struggle for Woman's Suffrage

THE CHEROKEE NATION: Life Before the Tears

PRIDE AND PROMISE: The Harlem Renaissance

EVOLUTION ON TRIAL (The Scopes Trial and Beyond)

THE MANHATTAN PROJECT: A Secret Wartime Mission

THE SHOT HEARD 'ROUND THE WORLD: The Beginnings of the American Revolution

THE PURCHASE OF ALASKA: Folly or Bargain?

ALL THAT GLITTERS: The Men and Women of the Gold and Silver Rushes

WOMEN IN THE CIVIL WAR: Warriors, Patriots, Nurses, and Spies

WESTWARD EXPANSION: Exploration & Settlement

CRY "WITCH": The Salem Witchcraft Trials - 1692

IRON HORSES ACROSS AMERICA: The Transcontinental Railroad

RECONSTRUCTION: Binding the Wounds

LIFE IN THE AMERICAN COLONIES: Daily Lifestyles of the Early Settlers

COLONIAL TRIANGULAR TRADE: An Economy Based on Human Misery

THE GREAT DEPRESSION: A Nation in Distress

THE NEW DEAL: Hope for the Nation

PRINCIPLES OF DEMOCRACY: The Constitution and the Bill of Rights